BIND UP YOUR BROKEN HEART

WHEN OTHERS FAIL US, WE CAN FIND HEALING WITH THE LORD.

Timothy J. Clarke

Published by Warner Press Inc.
Warner Press and the Warner Press logo are trademarks of Warner Press Inc.

Scripture quotations are from the King James Version (public domain).

Warner Press Inc.
PO Box 2499
Anderson, IN 46018-2499
800-741-7721
www.warnerpress.org

ISBN: 978-1-59317-879-6

Cover and layout by Curtis D.Corzine

Printed in the United States of America.

Endorsements

Bishop Timothy Clarke, scribe and prolific orator, has penned the consummate message of reassurance: when all else fails, remember the one who can Bind Up Your Broken Heart. *Hear ye him as he unveils to us the many ways God can use his Word to heal, restore, and bandage the wounds that come through the vicissitudes none of us can escape from. You will be richly blessed and strengthened for this journey of life.*

—Bishop T. D. Jakes
C.E.O., TDJ Enterprises
New York Times Best-Selling Author

"All of us experience times in life that are heart-breaking, disappointing, and painful. In Bind Up Your Broken Heart, *Bishop Clarke is at his best as he offers powerful and practical help. He equips, empowers, and encourages believers to be Spirit-filled overcomers. A great read! I highly recommend it."*

—Pastor Miki Merritt
Presiding Elder, National Association of the Church of God

"Timothy Clarke is an extraordinary expositor of God's Word, an outstanding pastor and shepherd, and a dynamic teacher and preacher. Grounded in the Scriptures and anointed by the Spirit, he knows how to bring light and life home. Reading Bind Up Your Broken Heart *is the next best thing to hearing Tim speak in person—and, in a way, even better: with this book in hand, you can revisit and study the truth that sets us free."*

—Rev. Jim Lyon
General Director, Church of God Ministries

"Bishop Clarke gives helpful insight to let us know that failure is not final—that God can move us from brokenness to blessedness, from tribulation to triumph, and from gloom to glory. This book can help you mature in your emotional and spiritual health by the grace of God."

—Rev. Michael A. Smith
Lead Pastor, Community Church of God, Atlanta, Georgia

"In a day of pulpit trivia, how spiritually refreshing to read the thoughts of one who dares to deal with something we all wrestle with—pain. Bishop Clarke invites us to journey with him through the Scriptures, that we might seek answers to one of life's most perplexing realities."

—Dr. Charles E. Booth
Senior Pastor, Mt. Olivet Baptist Church, Columbus, Ohio

CONTENTS

DEDICATION

The year 2016 marks the centennial celebration for the National Association of the Church of God, headquartered in West Middlesex, Pennsylvania, at a place affectionately known as "Zions Hill."

There is no way to adequately measure the impact of this group and its people upon me. So much of my life has been lived "under the gaze of the saints." Lessons learned, sermons sounded, songs sung, friendships formed, and faith forged are just some of the gifts given to me by and because of the National Association. I can truly say and sing with the songwriter, "O church of God! I love thy courts."

The year 2017 will mark the 40th anniversary of my marriage to a young lady whom I courted on those same grounds at West Middlesex, watching as she worked in the ice cream stand and with her parents in the kitchen. I wooed and won her in great part at "Zion's Hill." For forty years she has been companion, confidant, and constant. My love for her now is so much wiser than it was forty years ago, but no less real or true.

This book is dedicated to the National Association of the Church of God and to Clytemnestra Lawson Clarke. You have both helped to make me who I am and I cannot imagine my life without either of you.

— Tim Clarke

ACKNOWLEDGEMENTS

No work, project, or endeavor is ever accomplished or achieved in a vacuum. Others help, and their contributions matter in ways that are often not recognized or realized. So, too, with this book. I owe so much to the staff at Warner Press, especially to Joe Allison, who first approached me about this project. To Regina Jackson, who made all the connections and followed up with and on me at times, and most of all to Kevin Stiffler, who took ideas, words, and sentences and made them make sense—thank you! None of this would have happened without you.

—Tim Clarke

FOREWORD

In August 2016, the National Association of the Church of God celebrates its 100th anniversary. The Association was officially organized in 1916, having existed as early as 1906 as the "Brothers and Sisters of Love," an autonomous group that envisioned the uniting of African-Americans who were migrating from the South in search of new beginnings and new opportunities. Soon after its incorporation, the National Association began to affiliate with the Church of God, Anderson, Indiana.

Today, the National Association of the Church of God is an organization of over 420 congregations committed to assisting and involving all persons regardless of age, ethnic background, creed, educational level, or economic status. The Association strives to be a loving, holy, intergenerational community of faith, pursuing biblical truth and uniting the church to transform the world for Christ, with a mission to support and nurture pastors, identify and mentor leaders, develop healthy, connected churches, and empower Spirit-filled servants to do the work of the kingdom of God.

The release of *Bind Up Your Broken Heart* was timed to coincide with the centennial celebration of the National Association of the Church of God, where the book's author, Bishop Timothy J. Clarke, has served in various leadership roles and continues to minister.

Of all the miracles God does, healing broken hearts is certainly among the greatest. Psalm 147:3 says of the Lord, "He healeth the broken in heart, and bindeth up their wounds." Throughout the Bible we read stories of men and women who were crushed in spirit: rejected, discouraged, broken, and even ridiculed by family and friends. But these stories also show us that when people or situations hurt us, God can use that experience to burn away impurities in our faith and temper our character. God will stand by you when your heart is broken. Others may fail you, but you can find healing with the Lord; he will *Bind Up Your Broken Heart*.

The chapters of this book were transcribed from a series of sermons Bishop Timothy J. Clarke delivered at First Church of God in Columbus, Ohio, over a series of recent months—sermons that focused on the healing God brings. Of course, this written text can never capture the spirit of the services where Bishop Clarke's messages were originally preached. But it does reflect the bishop's heart and passion and also the Holy Spirit who lives in him and works through him. Timothy Clarke loves the Lord, he loves people, and he loves those particular people God uses him to minister to—whether it's in his own congregation, in the Columbus area, in the Berean Fellowship of Churches he founded, in the National Association of the Church of God, in the Church of God at large, or in any number of congregations where he visits to share the Word.

It is our prayer at Warner Press that God will speak through the words of this book to minister grace to you and *Bind Up Your Broken Heart*.

—Kevin Stiffler, editor
April 2016

CHAPTER 1:

When You Are Rejected (Joseph)

> And when they saw [Joseph] afar off, even before he came near unto them, [his brothers] conspired against him to slay him. And they said to one another, Behold, this dreamer cometh. Come now therefore, and let us slay him, and cast him into some pit, and we will say, Some evil beast hath devoured him: and we shall see what will become of his dreams. —Genesis 37:18–20

Bible characters remind us that we are not alone in the struggles of life. We have ancestors in the faith who have not only gone before us but persevered through the very things we are experiencing now. The Bible's accounts of great men and women of faith demonstrate that the same God who was with them is with us now.

One of our greatest faith ancestors was a man named Joseph, whom we read about in Genesis 37—50. Joseph's story has much to say about growing in and through the painful places of life, especially the pain of rejection. Almost from the moment of his birth, Joseph had to deal with rejection by his brothers. Much of it was brought on by their father, Jacob, who made no attempt to hide the fact that Joseph was his favorite among the sons. Genesis 37:4 says that when Joseph was still a boy, his brothers "hated him, and could not speak peaceably unto him." From that point through much of his life, Joseph had to deal with the pain of rejection.

Joseph's story teaches us that God can use anything and everything—even painful things—to mature us and make us better. God works not only through the pleasant and enjoyable experiences of life, but also through the negative things, the "bad stuff" that we don't want to experience. God can use it all to build our character and develop our spiritual fitness to serve him.

When people in your life
hurt you
and hate you
and try to stop you,
God is able to make your enemies your footstool (see Psalm 110:1) **and make them leave you alone.** No matter who your enemies are or how powerful they seem to be, God is able to take everything they do and make it work for your good (Romans 8:28).

Consider the entire story of Joseph. **Despite suffering rejection again and again**
from his brothers,
from Mr. and Mrs. Potiphar,
and from Pharaoh's butler,
Joseph emerged better than before. As old folks say, what doesn't kill you will make you stronger! I'm convinced that Joseph's story reveals some blessings and benefits that can come to us especially when we know the pain of rejection.

You Can Be Resilient

First, rejection can make you *resilient*. We must read the entire story of Joseph in Genesis 37—50 to get the full scope of what happened in his life, just as we have to read the entire story of Job to understand what God did in his life. The first chapter is not the end of either man's story.

When someone rejects you, you can be tempted to assume that one incident sums up the whole story, when

it's not even a chapter in your life;

it's not even a page in your life;

it's not even a paragraph in your life.

The rejection you have suffered may not even be *one line* in your life's story. In fact, it is only as important as you make it. Say to yourself, **"After the way those people treated me, after the way they dissed me,**

they're not worthy of a paragraph,

they're not worthy of a page,

they're not worthy of a chapter in my life!"

The sooner you put a period instead of a comma at the end of the sentence, the sooner you can start writing something better. Remember your punctuation! **Don't keep putting commas in your life story, such as,**

"They hurt me,"

"They left me,"

"They did me wrong,"

"They cheated me,"

and so on. Stop putting commas after the acts of jokers who mean you no good. Put a period after what they did and start writing another line. Write a new chapter of your life that does not include them. Say nothing more about them. **Let God take those people**

out of your mind,

out of your heart,

and out of your life.

You have been giving your enemies all the pages in your life, using all your ink to tell their part of your story, when it's time to turn the page and write another line.

There are many times in Joseph's story when we wonder how he would manage to bounce back. Again and again, his adversaries put him in a position where it seemed impossible for him to recover.

His brothers throw him in a pit,
...and we wonder, "How will he get out?"
His brothers sell him into slavery,
...and we wonder, "How will he get back to his father?"
Mrs. Potiphar accuses him of sexual assault,
...and we wonder, "How will he clear his name?"
A prisoner whom he helps to free forgets about him,
...and we wonder, "How will he ever gain his own freedom?"

But every time life deals Joseph a blow, he surprises us. Every time we think he is "down for the count," he gets back up. He's like the toys that used to be advertised, "They weeble and they wobble, but they don't fall down!" Joseph shows us that if we have faith in God, he will make us resilient, no matter how many times we are rejected.

If you are resilient, you keep coming back because you won't give your adversary the satisfaction of seeing you defeated. Don't count resilient people out, because the moment you think you've seen the last of them, they come right back.

Remember the TV action series called *MacGyver*? That fellow could use a piece of dental floss and a paper clip to get out of anything. If someone tries to push you into a corner—and they will—just say, "My middle name is MacGyver. I know you've blocked all the exits and closed all the windows and shut all the ventilation ducts. I know you expect to smother me with your rejection; but by the power of God, I am resilient. I will find a way back!"

Resilient people know *why* they want to get back up. I once attended a church board meeting where our lay leaders were trying to solve an especially difficult problem, and the chairman asked if I wanted to say anything else. "Just this," I replied. "When your 'why' is right, the 'how' works itself out." It's true. When your "why" is big enough, the "how" will always be found.

Too often we feel frustrated because we try to figure out the "how" first of all:

How am I going to make it?

How will I pay the bills?

How will I graduate from school?

How can I possibly...?

That word *how* has us confused. *How* keeps us from sleeping at night. *How* discourages us from trying. We need to focus on our *why*, because when the *why* is big enough, we can always figure out *how*.

Take a single mother who needs to provide for her family. When that mama knows her children are the *why*, she won't stop until she finds a *how*.

She may have to work two jobs,

***...but she will find a way* how.**

She may have to wear the same dress every Sunday,

***...but she will find a way* how.**

When the *why* is important enough, this woman will find a way *how*. She just needs a big enough reason to survive, an important enough reason to make it, and then the most amazing solutions appear.

If you ever say to yourself,

"I don't think I can take any more,"

"I don't think I can face another day,"

"I don't think I can bear another job being outsourced or downsized,"

or, "I'm just going to stay in bed and sleep my life away,"

then you need a better reason to live. If you find that reason, God will give you the strength to get out of bed, brush your teeth, wash your face, put on clean clothes, and go to another job interview. There will be days when you feel like quitting, when you feel too tired to go on. **But if you have a reason to live, something will rise up within you and say,**

"I have another fight in me.

I have another round in me.

I have another punch in me."

Then you'll pray, "God, give me strength!" and he will. If you have a big enough *why*, God will show you *how* to keep on fighting.

You Can Be Resourceful

Joseph's story also illustrates the fact that rejection, if handled properly, can make you *resourceful*. Whether in slavery, in prison, or in Potiphar's palace, Joseph learned to be resourceful. He was creative and imaginative in handling hardship. If you have plenty of personal cheerleaders, you don't need to know about this. **But if**

every time you trusted others,

...they hurt you;

and every time you handed your heart to other people,

...they stomped on it;

then you must be resourceful. You must learn to encourage yourself. Here's how Joseph did it.

Assess. First, Joseph knew what he had. He assessed his own resources, and so can you. Perhaps you don't have what someone else has, but you have what you need. Joseph had the ability to interpret dreams, which doesn't seem like much, but it took him to Pharaoh's palace.

Activate. Second, Joseph used what he had. He activated it.

- *Ray Kroc* was the man who made McDonald's restaurants famous. All he had were "two all-beef patties, special sauce, lettuce, cheese, pickles, onions on a sesame seed bun." But he used what he had and now McDonald's is everywhere.
- *Mary Kay Ash* had an idea about marketing cosmetics through women in their local neighborhoods. Now Mary Kay Cosmetics is a business worth billions of dollars.
- *Truett Cathy* used a simple chicken sandwich and some lemonade to revolutionize the way we eat chicken. His Chick-fil-A restaurant chain is now a household name.

We make these people gazillionaires; but if we studied their stories, we would be richer still. What made Ray, Mary, and Truett better than you? Nothing. The Bible says, "God is no respecter of persons" (Acts 10:34), so he did not give these people any special advantages over you. However, they used what they had—they activated it—to achieve great things.

Accentuate. Finally, Joseph made a specialty of what he had. He had the ability to interpret dreams, and he knew that everybody has dreams. So when people started to talk about dreams that puzzled or troubled them, Joseph volunteered to explain what they meant.

Every chance you get, every time others say something germane to your ability, you ought to show them what you can do. You may start by volunteering, but if you really accentuate what you have for the benefit of others, they will realize they can't afford to do without you. If you make yourself valuable, people will pay you what you're worth. That's what Joseph did again and again, and he eventually became Pharaoh's right-hand man.

You Can Develop Resolve

I have read Joseph's life story many times, and I am amazed to see his *resolve*—how he didn't give up. If you threw me in a pit, sold me into slavery, locked me in solitary confinement, I would be sorely tempted to surrender to the circumstances. But if you have ever been rejected as Joseph was, you know you can't give up. This may mean nothing to you now because you have never experienced rejection on this heartbreaking level.

You've been cute all your life.
You've always had plenty of friends.
You've always had a decent job.

But if you belong to the Reject Club, as I do, you know a powerful secret. You know why a rejected person can never give up. Here's why: if you give up, it means your enemies have won.

If your mother or father abandons you,
if your spouse leaves you,
if your brothers and sisters throw you out,

you don't give up because that would mean they were right, and you were wrong.

Rejection puts a steel-like resolve within you. That resoluteness comes from your pain. If you've sat alone in your room while your friends were outside playing, if you've not been invited when everyone else went to the mall, if you've been passed over for job promotions time and again, you can let that rejection give birth to a passionate resolve to overcome. In your worst moments, you make a promise to yourself.

When you cry yourself to sleep,
when team members will not talk to you,
when no boy or girl will pay attention to you,

you make yourself a promise. Because it's forged in the blast furnace of pain, you know it can never be broken. **You promise yourself,**

"I'm going to be somebody,
I'm going to rise above this,
I'm going to survive,

because I know God has something better for me." His Word says, "Weeping may endure for a night, but joy cometh in the morning" (Psalm 30:5b). Whatever it takes, however long it takes, I will survive because I belong to God.

If you are a member of the Reject Club, banish the word *quit* from your vocabulary. Let rejection make you *resilient*, *resourceful*, and *resolved*—but don't let it make you quit.

Remember what Joseph's brothers said when they threw him into that miserable pit? "We shall see what will become of his dreams" (Genesis 37:20). What will you let other people do to *your* dreams? **When you are rejected,**

are you going to give in?
Are you going to capitulate?
Are you going to abort your dreams?

Or are you going to pursue them? Only you can decide.

CHAPTER 2:

When You Are Broken (Woman with an Issue of Blood)

And a woman having an issue of blood twelve years, which had spent all her living upon physicians, neither could be healed of any, Came behind him, and touched the border of his garment: and immediately her issue of blood stanched. And Jesus said, Who touched me? When all denied, Peter and they that were with him said, Master, the multitude throng thee and press thee, and sayest thou, Who touched me? And Jesus said, Somebody hath touched me: for I perceive that virtue is gone out of me. And when the woman saw that she was not hid, she came trembling, and falling down before him, she declared unto him before all the people for what cause she had touched him, and how she was healed immediately. And he said unto her, Daughter, be of good comfort: thy faith hath made thee whole; go in peace. —Luke 8:43–48

In this passage we meet a nameless woman whose story teaches us that God will meet you in a place of brokenness. This woman had suffered with an issue of blood for twelve years. There was no clinic, no urgent care, no emergency room. There was no Affordable Care Act saying she could not be denied because of preexisting conditions. In fact, there was no health insurance at all. The text says she had spent all that she had. She was already broken in her fitness, and now she had become broken in her finances. There was no money left. **The woman had spent**

all of her savings,

all of her investments,

all of her retirement money,

all of her shoe money.

The rainy-day money was gone. All her money in the cookie jar, all the money her mama told her to hide from her husband in case he acted crazy—all of it was gone. She had spent it all. She had gone to every doctor, and she had nothing to show for it. At this point her only prospects were to get better or die.

There are so many women who are broken in their finances. You married a guy who took advantage of you, lied to you, didn't tell you he was in debt up to his eyeballs, ran up your credit cards, then left you. Now you've got to pay all the bills. Or maybe you made a bad choice, or found yourself in a situation beyond your control. You were laid off or fired, or the company downsized or moved overseas—whatever it is. And now your finances are broken. The passage tells us that all of this woman's money was gone. She was in a tough place.

More Than Your Money

I once met a lady whose finances were broken, and she told me something I'll never forget. She said, "Preacher, when the money all ran out, I finally saw that I was more than my money. I realized that I might not have any money—but I still have me. I looked in the mirror and said to myself, 'You may be broke, but you're still somebody.' "

Sometimes your money will get funny. **But when all the money is gone, remember that**

you are more than your money.

You are more than your bank account.

You are more than your bottom line.

We need to affirm the fact that our money, our wallet, our credit cards are not what make us.

This lady also told me, "I found out the hard way that you'd better learn how to *manage* your money. You need to stop running through money like Sherman ran through Georgia. You'd better learn how to save your money, how to manage your money, how to maximize your money. You'd better learn how to have some delayed gratification and tell yourself no, because hard times may be coming, and if you spend it all when things are going well, you won't have any left when things go bad."

Some of you are going through money like it's water. You're buying everything for everybody, taking folks on vacation, taking them on a cruise. But you had better watch who you take. Some people will act like your friend, but they will go and lie about you and talk about you while they're spending your money.

This lady told me one other thing. She said, "I learned that you're more than your money, and I learned that you need to know how to manage your money. And I also learned that there are some things money can't buy."

Money can buy medicine and doctor's appointments and counseling,

...but it can't always buy healing.

Money can buy you a bed,

...but not sleep.

Money can buy you food,

...but not an appetite.

Money can buy you a house,

...but not a home.

Money may buy you some "hangers-on,"

...but it won't buy you real friends.

There are some things money can't buy.

Keep the Faith!

You might be broken in your fitness and broken in your finances. **You might be**

jacked up,

tore up,

messed up,

broke,

busted,

and disgusted.

Your body might be broken and your money might be broken. But no matter what else is broken in your life, if you keep your faith intact, you're going to be all right.

The woman in this passage had an issue of blood for twelve years. For 4,380 days she had been sick. She had spent all that she had and hadn't gotten any better. Her fitness was broken and her finances were broken, but she heard that Jesus was coming to town and that he was a healer who had more healing in the hem of his garment than all of the doctors put together.

She got up that morning and said to herself, "You have been sick for 4,380 days, but I've got a feeling that everything's going to be all right." They tell you in school that you shouldn't talk to yourself, that it's a sign of neurosis or psychosis or something else. But sometimes if you want to stay sane you'd better talk to yourself. This woman said to herself, "If I can just touch the hem of his garment, I will be made whole."

Perhaps it was early when she awoke, still dark outside, and her husband asked her where she was going. He figured maybe she had a doctor's appointment. She made her way feebly out of bed and got dressed, thinking how much weight she had lost. Her clothes didn't even fit anymore. They used to be so snug and accentuate the positive; now they hung off her like a shirt on a hanger. But she put her clothes on and started walking down the street. Every now and then she would have to stop and catch her breath because the weakness in her body was compounded by the financial stress. The whole way she kept telling herself, "If I can just touch the hem of his garment, I will be made whole."

When she got there, there was a crowd. She had thought that by getting up early, she would be the first one there. But there must have been some other desperate folks in the city besides her. And her first thought was, "Give up. Go back home and try it another day." But somebody had said that Jesus was only passing by on *this* day. So she decided that she had to be all in.

Instead of just walking up to Jesus, she dropped to her knees and started crawling because all she needed was to touch the hem of his garment.

She didn't need to talk to him eyeball-to-eyeball.

She didn't need a conversation face-to-face.

What she needed was down there.

So she got down on the ground and made her way up. She made her way to where she thought he was and she saw the phylacteries hanging from his robe and she said, "I think that's him," and with one thrust she reached out and touched him. And the moment she made contact with the hem of his garment, something like electricity shot through her, and she found herself standing up. She felt energy that she had never felt before coursing through her body. She felt strength, vigor, and vitality that she hadn't felt in 4,379 days.

She knew in her heart that she had been healed. She was getting ready to shout when Jesus turned around and said, "Who touched me?"

And the disciples said, "Wait a minute. There's a crowd of people, everybody's milling around. What do you mean, who touched you?"

Jesus said, "You see, that's your problem. You're always thinking in the earthly realm.

I didn't say someone brushed up against me.

I didn't say someone rubbed up on me.

I said, somebody touched me—

and when that person touched me, virtue went out of me."

And that woman stood up and said, "I don't know how to tell you, but it was me. I've been sick for 4,380 days. I was at the end of my rope. Yes, it was me who touched him, but *Jesus* touched *me*. 'O He touched me, And O the joy that floods my soul; Something happened, and now I know, He touched me and made me whole.'"[1]

My Own Journey

My mama's in heaven now. But I watched my mother, without a man in her life, raise her children. She didn't have a bunch of men in and out of the house. She didn't have a bunch of men sleeping with her. She raised her children with the help of my grandmother. She made sure we were fed and that we had something to wear.

1. From "He Touched Me" by William J. Gaither. Copyright © 1992 Hanna Street Music (BMI) (adm. at CapitolCMGPublishing.com). All rights reserved. Used by permission.

Let me tell you what God can do! The Lord will make a way somehow. He'll put food on your table and clothes on your back. **But he'll also put gas in your car and a roof over your head...**

joy in your soul...

running in your feet...

clapping in your hands...

and praises in your mouth!

There were some times we didn't have anything to eat and my mama would make drop biscuits, with just a little syrup. That's all we had, but she told us that the Lord would make a way somehow. And I watched my mama and my grandmother, with a little bit of nothing, trust the Lord. I am so glad I came up the way I did, because I don't need a car to praise him. And I don't need a house to praise him. If I have Jesus, that's enough for me.

Faith will find a way when it looks like there is no way. Faith will find a way, and faith will fight. When it looks like the odds are against you, faith rolls up its sleeves and keeps on fighting. And if faith finds a way and faith keeps on fighting, then faith will find favor with God.

Maybe the situation before you seems impossible. But God specializes in things that seem impossible, and in the power of the Holy Ghost he can do want no one else can.

If you're sick,

...he's a healer.

If you're lost,

...he's the deliverer.

If you're bound,

...he's a liberator.

If you're down,

...he'll set you high up above your enemies.

If you're surrounded,
...he'll make a way out of nowhere.
If you're hungry,
...he's bread in a starving land.
If you're thirsty,
...he's water flowing out of the rock.
If you're sad,
...he's the joy and the lifter up of your head.
And if you're lonely,
...he's a friend who sticks closer than a brother.

He satisfies. Sure, he supplies. Life would be worthless without him. All things in Jesus I find. He walks with me. He talks with me.

I realize that brokenness can be a very painful topic. Whenever you talk about brokenness it causes people to take a look at their own lives and remember their own broken places, and sometimes that hurts.

A dear friend and brother of mine wrote a book called *Stronger in My Broken Places*. Just like the title says, it talks about how, when you allow God to heal you, he can make you stronger at those places where you were broken. In fact, you can even *dance* with legs that have been broken! And that's what I want for you. I really want you to believe that you're going to come back from this, that there is healing beyond your hurt. There are blessings beyond your brokenness. I want you to believe it, because if you do, then it can give you hope, but if you don't believe it then you're going to despair. God meets us in unlikely places, and one of those places is the place of our brokenness. So I just simply want to encourage you to allow God to minister health and help and healing to your life.

I know all of us are broken in some place, and in some way. **But God is the healer of**

broken fitness,

broken finances,

broken hearts,

***broken* anything—**

if you will just have faith. There is worship beyond the wound, there is help beyond the hurt, and there is praise beyond the pain.

CHAPTER 3:

When You Are Shamed (David's Men)

> And it came to pass after this, that the king of the children of Ammon died, and Hanun his son reigned in his stead. Then said David, I will shew kindness unto Hanun the son of Nahash, as his father shewed kindness unto me. And David sent to comfort him by the hand of his servants for his father. And David's servants came into the land of the children of Ammon. And the princes of the children of Ammon said unto Hanun their lord, Thinkest thou that David doth honour thy father, that he hath sent comforters unto thee? hath not David rather sent his servants unto thee, to search the city, and to spy it out, and to overthrow it? Wherefore Hanun took David's servants, and shaved off the one half of their beards, and cut off their garments in the middle, even to their buttocks, and sent them away. When they told it unto David, he sent to meet them, because the men were greatly ashamed: and the king said, Tarry at Jericho until your beards be grown, and then return.
>
> —2 Samuel 10:1–5

Have you ever done anything you're ashamed of? We all have. I know I have. And I suspect that you have as well. Let's be honest, there are few things in life more painful than when something has happened to us that shames us. Or when we have done something of which we are ashamed.

There is life on the other side of shame. You don't have to stay stuck in it. You don't have to live there forever.

The God we serve,

the God we worship,

the God who made us

is a God who heals us—not only of our sin, but also of our shame.

You don't have to walk around with your head down.

You don't have to walk around with your shoulders drooping.

You don't have to walk around with your eyes darting from one person to another.

You don't have to walk around ashamed to look others straight in the eye.

The God whom we serve and the God whom we worship is a God who is able to help you lift up your head and square your shoulders. **You can live life fully and freely**

in spite of what you've been through,

in spite of what you've done.

and in spite of what may have been done to you.

Our God is a God of restoration who can bring you out, bring you through, bring you back so that shame does not have to haunt you all of your life.

Some of us have lived with shame.

Shame of where we were born.

Shame of our family.

Shame of* how *we were born.

Shame of things we didn't have.

Shame of how we live.
Shame of things we've done.
Or shame from things done to us.

Perhaps it was
an uncle,
a cousin,
a father,
a stepfather,
a babysitter,
a Boy Scout leader,
or a preacher.

Somebody
hurt you,
misused you,
abused you,
scarred you,

and you've been living with shame. But I have good news for you. There is a God who is able to heal you from that shame. There is a God who is able to give you the ability to stand back up again. No matter what you've been through, God is still able.

David's Men

In 2 Samuel 10 we meet some men who suffered an experience in their lives that caused them shame. They encountered this shame on a mission for their king. They were mistreated, humiliated, and embarrassed. They had their beards shaved off. Their garments were cut, exposing their private parts. And they were sent away shamed.

Some of you have been mistreated and then sent away shamed. You only went to bed with him because you thought he loved you. Or you slept with her and then she got up and didn't even remember your name. That person never called you again, just left you with shame. You had said, "I'm going to get through college and not sleep around. I'm going to start fresh. I'm going to get me a new job and start all over. I'm not going to repeat the same sick behavior that I once did." But then you found yourself right back there. And someone walked away from you, and left you shamed. I want to look at how we can bounce back from that kind of shame.

The text says that when David heard about what happened to his men, he told them to stay in Jericho until their beards grew back, and then to return. There it is. **If you and I are going to beat shame, if we're not going to allow shame to**

rule us,

run us,

and run amok in our lives,

then we have to do what those men did.

We've got to find a place to retreat, a time to regroup, and then we have to ask God to give us the power to return. You might be saying, "Pastor, I don't want to hear that. I don't want to be bothered.

I've been hurt so bad,

I've been wounded so deeply,

I've been so emotionally scarred,

I don't want to return." But here's what I want to tell you: *if you don't return, they win.* And you can't let them win. You have to find the power to return.

You Can't Hide Forever

When you've known shame or when you have been shamed, you cannot hide forever. The temptation and the tendency is to want to run as far away as possible. You never want to look back, much less go back. But you can't hide forever.

David told his men, "I'm going to send you to Jericho. That's a place you can retreat, where you can stay until your beards grow back. There will be a period of time for you to regroup, but I expect you to return at some point. You are not staying in Jericho. Go there as long as you need to go. Stay as long as you need to stay, but it is only temporary, not permanent. I expect that at some point you will get back to life. You will report for duty. You will show back up here because God will give you the power to return."

Some of you have been at Jericho long enough. You need to ask God today to give you the power to get up, and leave Jericho, and go on with your life.

Jericho was a safe place,
it was a necessary place,
it was a good place,
but it's not your place.

David said to these men, "You stay in Jericho until your beards grow back, and then you return." You cannot hide forever.

Some of you have been hiding too long.

Your shame has imprisoned you,
your pain has arrested you,
your disgrace has encased you.

And you're living in your shame when you ought to be living in victory. It's time for you to come out of hiding. You've been hiding behind excuses all of this time. You could have been married years ago, but you're hiding behind the pain of that old relationship. God says, "I've sent you somebody to love you. But you're hiding and you're making excuses. And because you're doing that, you can't step into what I have for you."

You cannot hide forever. Whenever you try to hide, you really seek to escape and avoid three things. The first one is *reality*. Sometimes you run into people who are always hiding, always dodging, always ducking, always running. Here's what they're dealing with: They don't want to face reality. They don't want to deal with what happened to them. They've tried to paint it different, make it different—it was not there, it didn't happen like that, it didn't go down that way. People who talk like that can never get healed. We cannot be healed until we are willing to face reality.

You were abused, you were molested, you were abandoned, you were neglected, you were hurt. But the operative term is *was*. That is not you *now*. That's not the whole story of your life. But you can never get past that until you deal with the reality of it. When you and I hide, we are often running from reality.

When you try to hide forever, you're not only running from reality, but you are also trying to run from *responsibility*. What happened to you was not your fault. That incident is not your responsibility, but what *is* your responsibility is your *response* to what happened to you. You should never give your abuser the power to determine how you will respond. Don't give the person who hurt you the power to determine your response!

You are responsible for your response. And you are able to respond the right way because "greater is he that is in you, than he that is in the world" (1 John 4:4). If Christ is in your life, he gives you the ability to assume responsibility. I'm not saying what happened is your responsibility. But what *is* your responsibility is how you respond from this day forward. When you try to hide, you hide from reality—"It didn't really happen" or "It didn't happen like *that*." Or you hide from responsibility—responsibility for your response.

When you try to hide forever, you're not only running from reality and running from responsibility, but you are also trying to avoid *re-entry*. This means that you never get back in the game.

You got fouled,
you missed the shot,
you fumbled the ball,
and the coach pulled you out. He said to sit on the bench, and you're sitting there collecting splinters on your backside. What you ought to be doing is saying, "Coach, put me back in!"

You can't hide forever. You can't avoid reality and you can't avoid responsibility, and at some point it's time for re-entry. After a certain period, it's time for you to get back in the game. For some people it's a couple of months, for some it's a year, for some it's several years, depending on what they've gone through. Only you and God know how long that period needs to be. But at some point, it has to end.

David said, "Stay in Jericho until…" Then he said to return. It was not permanent for his men. It should not be permanent for us, either. You can't hide forever.

Letting Go of the Past

Not only can you not hide forever, but you cannot hold on to the past forever, either. There comes a point in your life where you have to let it go.
There will be a time when
you have to process it,
you have to deal with it,
and then you have to let it go.
If you hold on to your past forever—if you don't give that thing to God, whatever it is—then you give the person who shamed you too much power.

Back in 2013, three young ladies in Cleveland who had been kidnapped by a demonic, demented man and held captive for several years were finally rescued. Now that they're physically free, they are no longer in that house anymore. But you'd better believe that the memories are still there. The nightmares are still there. The horror is still there. It will take years for them to heal. But here is what they must do. At some point, place, and period they must learn how to release that to God. If they don't, even though they are free their captor will still have power over their lives.

Whoever hurt you,
whoever abused you,
whoever molested you,
whoever mistreated you—

that person is not worthy of having power over your life ten, fifteen, or twenty years later. Cut him loose. Shut him off, and do not let him ruin your life forever.

When you don't let go of your past and your pain and your shame, you give the person who hurt you too much power. You also give the *period* in which the incident happened too much power, as well—that time in your life when you were teenagers, when you were a young girl, when you were a young boy, whenever it happened. That was just a *period* in your life. But the Enemy is an expert at taking a period and making it permanent. You end up living all of your life out of the poison of that period. That stretch of two years, five years, ten years, whatever it was—that period of life now becomes your whole life. And life was never meant to be lived boxed in by a period.

That was a *season* in your life. But always remember that seasons change. That was the winter of your life. It was a difficult, dark, terrible place, but you can rejoice in the fact that winter doesn't last all year. You may have been in winter but you're about to step into spring, and after spring comes summer.

Your winter is over,
your spring is here,
and your summer is coming.

Step into a new season. Do not let that past period of your life be your whole life.

Too many people have allowed a period of their lives to have too much power. They have been stunted and stymied by something that happened to them when they were nine. And now they are 40. Or 60. And that ugly period still rules their lives. How much life have you missed? Do you know how much has happened in life that you missed out on because you got stuck in a period? Your season is about to change. The only question is, are you ready to step into your new season?

When you cling to the past you give the person who hurt you too much power. You give that period of your life too much power. And you give the *pain* of that time too much power, as well. Here's what I mean by that. Whatever happened to you that brought you shame—whether it was self-inflicted or imposed by somebody else—you cannot let the pain of that shame become your constant companion.

The reason the pain stays with you is because you keep reliving the incident and rehearsing it and rehashing it instead of releasing it and giving it to God.

So you can rehearse it,
relive it,
and rehash it,
or you can release it.

Once you release it, the pain of that time doesn't have power over you anymore. The memory may still be there. But you will be able to look back over your life and remember those times, and they won't hurt you like they used to. In fact, you can look back and say, "It could have taken me out, but because God was with me, it's only a reminder now."

Like David's men, your beard will grow again. I know some of you reading this are ladies, but you get the point. You will smile again. Your joy will return.

> ***There's going to come a morning***
>
> ***...when you will wake up and greet the day with excitement and enthusiasm.***
>
> ***There's going to come a day***
>
> ***...when it won't hurt as bad as it hurts right now.***
>
> ***God will heal you***
>
> ***...and allow you to come back from where you've been.***

God is going to heal you. You might not feel that right now because the pain of the memory is so real and it's so present and it's so powerful. "Weeping may endure for a night, but joy cometh in the morning" (Psalm 30:5). You can be healed. You can be, and you will be, because God is a healer of the broken places in our lives.

Have faith that when God heals you, you're going to make a comeback.

CHAPTER 4:

When It's Hard to Let Go (Prodigal Family)

A certain man had two sons: And the younger of them said to his father, Father, give me the portion of goods that falleth to me. And he divided unto them his living. And not many days after the younger son gathered all together, and took his journey into a far country, and there wasted his substance with riotous living. And when he had spent all, there arose a mighty famine in that land; and he began to be in want....And when he came to himself, he said, How many hired servants of my father's have bread enough and to spare, and I perish with hunger! I will arise and go to my father, and will say unto him, Father, I have sinned against heaven, and before thee, And am no more worthy to be called thy son: make me as one of thy hired servants. And he arose, and came to his father....The father said to his servants, Bring forth the best robe, and put it on him; and put a ring on his hand, and shoes on his feet: And bring hither the fatted calf, and kill it; and let us eat, and be merry....Now his elder son was in the field: and as he came and drew nigh to the house, he heard musick and dancing. And he called one of the servants, and asked what these

things meant. And he said unto him, Thy brother is come; and thy father hath killed the fatted calf, because he hath received him safe and sound. And he was angry, and would not go in. —Luke 15:11–28a

---

This parable in Luke 15 is one of the most well-known and most beloved parables of Jesus. It's the parable of the prodigal son. The son who determined and decided to leave home, to leave his father's house and go live in a far and foreign country.

If you and I are honest, we will admit that one of the hardest things in life is to let go.

It's hard to let go of your children,
hard to let go of relationships,
hard to let go of a career that's going nowhere,
hard to let go of memories and dreams.

Letting go is never easy. And yet, letting go is part of life and part of growing up. I find myself struggling in this area. I was born in New York. There is a saying (and I have personally found it to be true), "Once a New Yorker, always a New Yorker." New York is in my blood. But I've been gone from there so long now. So many of the people I knew and loved there are now gone themselves. And I'm realizing every year that this is a part of my life, my story, my journey that I have to let go of.

I'm probably never going to live in New York again. I just have to let it go. Letting go is never easy. But growing up demands letting go. And that's what we see in this parable. This young man comes of age, he leaves home, things go real bad, and he comes back home—and all along the story line there is this need to let go.

Holding Out versus Holding Back

When I look at the father in this story, it dawns on me that this dad had to let go of what he had been holding back. It's not that he had been holding *out* on his sons. He was holding *back* something for them. There is a big difference between holding out and holding back. But we don't always see that and we don't always understand it. We think that others are holding out on us, trying to deny us or cheat us of something, when in fact they're not holding something *out* on us; they're just holding something *back* for us.

Some of you are angry at people.

You're angry at your boss or your supervisor,

you're angry at your spouse,

or you're angry at your parents

because you feel that they are holding out on you. What I want to suggest is that maybe they're not holding something out on you. Maybe they are holding something *back* for you.

Let me put it this way. Some of us are angry at God. We feel like God is holding back on us. He's blessing here, he's blessing there, he's blessing this one, he's blessing that one. All around there are other folks getting blessed. **We wonder,**

When is* my *turn?

When is* my *time?

When is* my *break coming?

It seems that everybody you talk to is shouting about their blessings, excited over what God has done. And it looks as if God has forgotten your name, your number, and your address. He's blessing up and down the street, around the corner, and all over the neighborhood. But it seems that every time a blessing gets right to your door the UPS man from heaven drives right by and takes the package to your neighbor's house. And you get mad because you feel that God is holding out on you.

Before you cuss God out and get mad with God, consider that maybe God is not holding out—maybe he's holding something *back*. Maybe God has something so great and so good and so wonderful that you're not ready for it right now, but he's holding it for you.

He's not going to give it to somebody else.
He's not going to let somebody else have it.
He's getting it ready for you and getting you ready for it.

Are you mature enough to handle it?

A lot of stuff you think you want, you're not ready for yet. You can't handle it yet. You couldn't deal with it yet. But when God gets you where he wants you to be and where you need to be, he is going to give you what you ask for. In fact, he's not just going to give you what you ask for. God is getting ready to blow your mind and give you *more* than what you ask for. Because sometimes God saves the best for last. Others might seem to be getting it all—a job, a promotion, a scholarship, a spouse, a car, whatever. But as soon as God gets through blessing them, God's got something for you. God's not holding out. He's holding back.

You've been wondering what's up with God—why God is taking so long, why God is so slow. But he's actually helping you. It's not that God is holding out on you, he's holding something back for you.

What God has for you must be fabulous.
What God has for you must be fantastic.
What God has for you must be getting ready
to blow your mind

because it's taken so long and you've had to wait this long. If God's had you in a holding pattern all this time, what's coming must be getting ready to blow your mind. Because God never holds out; he just holds back.

God's holding something back for you—for as soon as you grow up.

As soon as you get ready,
as soon as you take the training wheels off your bicycle,
as soon as you get some real shoes,
as soon as you get out of your diapers and start wearing real clothes,
God's got something for you.

God is not holding out on you. He's holding something back for you. What the father had was going to be that boy's anyhow. What the boy asked for was going to be his sooner or later. He just couldn't wait for it. And that's what messes a lot of us up. A whole lot of us rush ahead of God and get stuff we're not ready for.

Some of you should admit that you weren't ready for your first marriage. In fact, chances are that your second marriage should have been your first marriage. You went and jumped ahead of God and married somebody when you weren't ready to be married. But aren't you glad God gave you a second chance? Because even when you jump out of line, he'll let you come back around and get back in line until it's your turn. So stay in line!

The boy's father had to let go of what he was holding back. He had it for the son all the time. He was saving it for the son. But the son wanted it before he was ready. How do I know he wasn't ready? Because the text says that he wasted it. How many of us have wasted stuff? How many of us got stuff before we were ready for it, before we were mature enough to handle it? And we ended up wasting it.

The father wasn't holding out; he was holding back.

Letting Go of Brokenness

I also notice in this story that the younger son had to let go of his brokenness. The father had to let go of what he was holding back. And the younger boy, the prodigal, had to let go of his brokenness. Now, we're not told how long the son was gone, whether it was weeks, or months, or years. We don't know how long. But here's what we do know. He was gone long enough to run out of money. It doesn't take long to do that in our own day and time. However long he was out there, life and people, false friends, fake friends caused great damage, and in order to come back home he had to let go of the experiences of life that had broken him.

We hear a lot today about post-traumatic stress disorder. Many of those returning from combat are wounded warriors, and the wounds are not always just physical. Some of our soldiers—men and women, young people who have gone off to fight in Iraq and in Afghanistan and in other parts of the Middle East—come back suffering from post-traumatic stress disorder. They have flashbacks and dreams and nightmares, memories of combat and war that break them.

Some of you know that your marriage has given you post-traumatic stress. Your job has given you post-traumatic stress. Sometimes even coming to church—getting involved with some folks in the church—will give you post-traumatic stress.

A divorce can break you.

A failed business can break you.

An unrealized dream can break you.

There are a lot of broken people around us, but there comes a point in our lives where we have to let it go. I know the dude messed you over. I know he messed you up and jacked up your credit. I know he ran the bills up and walked out. I feel sorry for you. But I've got to say this. You should have known it was coming when you married him without him having a job.

I know he messed you over. I know she hurt you. I know you're reeling and rocking from the damage and the devastation of the divorce, but here's what I want to tell you.

If you're going to be whole,
if you're going to be healed,
if you're ever going to walk in newness of life,
you've got to let the brokenness go. You've got to forgive him, you've got to forget her, and you've got to move on. You cannot live your life filled with rancor and vengeance, always thinking, "I've got to get him back! I've got to show her!" You've got to stop all that. You can't make every decision in your life about that person. At some point you've got to declare, "You did me wrong, you did me dirty, and it wasn't right, but I'm over it, and I'm going to go on and live my life, and I am going to let it go."

There comes a point where you've got to let go of the broken places in your life.

Letting Go of Bitterness

Oftentimes when we read this parable, we overlook the older son. The father had to let go of the stuff he was holding back. The younger son had to let go of his brokenness. But there was also something that older boy had to let go of. He had to let go of his bitterness. Now remember, this is a parable—a story that employs human, earthly images to teach a spiritual message. In the parable, we pretty quickly see that the father represents God and the younger son represents publicans and sinners. But guess who the older son is? Church folks.

The older boy represented the Pharisees and scribes of Jesus' day. This son was filled with bitterness toward the father for still loving the younger son.

And he was bitter with his brother for leaving in the first place. In fact, he was so angry and so bitter that he would not even go in and join the party when the younger brother came back home. Jesus implied that this is the condition of some church folks who get mad because God the Father still loves sinners.

Here's the bottom line. There are a lot of people who are bitter—not because of what other folks have done but because of what the Father has done. You can't figure out why God hasn't punished your ex-spouse. Every time you see him, you are hoping for signs of some debilitating disease. And that joker walks in just as healthy as ever. Every recital, every softball game, you hope he will come in limping. But he comes in strutting. And you can't figure it out. *God, if you're on my side, why won't you get him, why won't you get her, why won't you—my boss, my coworker, the person who lied about me, who mistreated me, who misrepresented me—why won't you do something to let that person know you're on my side?* But here's what I need you to know. If you don't let go of the bitterness, God can never bless you.

That older son was so bitter. But here's what I don't understand. If you look at the first part of the story, it tells us that the younger son said to the father, "Give me. Give me the portion that belongs to me." The next line says that the father divided it unto *them*. He asked for his. The father gave him his and gave the older son his too. Which means the boy got mad over nothing. It wasn't like the father gave the younger son something he didn't give the older son when he divided the estate. He gave them both their portion even though the older son didn't ask.

Here's what I'm trying to say. Instead of tripping over how God is blessing somebody else, would you wake up and smell the coffee and realize how God's been blessing *you*?

I may not have everything I want,

...but I've got more than what I deserve.

I may not be driving a brand-new car,

...but at least I have reliable transportation.

I may not be living in the best house,

...but at least I've got a roof over my head.

I may not be wearing designer clothes,

...but at least I've got clothes on my back.

I may not be eating filet mignon,

...but at least I've got three square meals a day.

I may not be a millionaire,

...but at least I've got some money in my pocket and some gas in my car.

God is still blessing me.

I'm not going to let the devil steal my praise.

I'm not going to let him steal my peace.

I'm not going to let him steal my joy.

Yes, some of my enemies are doing good, but I'm still blessed. Some of my haters may be doing good, but I'm still blessed. Somebody who hurt me may be doing good, but I'm still blessed. If I keep my heart right, the Lord will bless me more.

God will let your enemy live long enough to see you get blessed. "The LORD is my shepherd; I shall not want. He maketh me to lie down in green pastures: he leadeth me beside the still waters. He restoreth my soul.... Thou preparest a table before me in the presence of mine enemies" (Psalm 23:1–5). *Where* did you say the table was? The table is in the presence of my enemies. The only reason you've got an enemy is because God wants to show your enemy that he cannot stop you from getting blessed. **The fact that I have enemies means that**

the more they hate on me,
...the more God blesses me.
The more they dig ditches,
...the more God protects me.
The more they try to bring me down,
...the more the Lord God lifts me up.

God prepares a table for us in the presence of our enemies. This means all your enemies can do is sit there and watch you get blessed.

They can't touch you,
they can't stop you,
they can't hinder you,

because when God gets ready to bless you, there's nobody who can hold back the blessing. So go ahead and get blessed. **In the presence of your enemy,**

don't let your bitterness,
don't let your anger,
don't let your frustration

block your blessing.

"I will bless the LORD at all times; his praise shall continually be in my mouth" (Psalm 34:1).

The Lord will make a way for you,
the Lord will fight your battles,
the Lord will bring you out.

Whatever you're mad about, whatever you're angry about, whatever you're bitter about,

get rid of the bitterness and get some blessing.
Get rid of the cursing and get some celebration.
Get rid of the profanity and get some praise.

Things will happen when you praise the Lord. Things will change when you praise him. Heaven hears when you praise him. Joy returns. Let everything that has breath praise him. The way out is to praise your way out.

The father had to let go of what he was holding back. The younger son had to let go of his brokenness. And the older son had to let go of his bitterness. Blessings flow when you let go. Can you let go?

Perhaps you need to let some stuff go. I've been dealing with that recently. I realize that I'm never going back to New York. Never. And I just have to let it go. I don't care how nostalgic and homesick I get. The Lord told me that where I am now is home. You keep talking about your own "New York City." But New York is not your home. That's where you're *from*. You've got to let that season in your life go.

You've got to grow up and let some of the stuff in your life go. It's a sign of maturity when you can let it go. The father had to let go of what he was holding back. He had made an investment. He had accrued interest. He had an inheritance that he was holding back. There came a point to let it go. He divided unto them his estate, what he had been holding back. He had to say, "You know what? If these boys want it, even though I want better for them, I cannot want more for them than they want for themselves."

Sometimes we have to let it go.

CHAPTER 5:

When You Need Restoration (Samson)

And when Delilah saw that [Samson] had told her all his heart, she sent and called for the lords of the Philistines, saying, Come up this once, for he hath shewed me all his heart. Then the lords of the Philistines came up unto her, and brought money in their hand. And she made him sleep upon her knees; and she called for a man, and she caused him to shave off the seven locks of his head; and she began to afflict him, and his strength went from him. And she said, The Philistines be upon thee, Samson. And he awoke out of his sleep, and said, I will go out as at other times before, and shake myself. And he wist not that the Lord was departed from him. But the Philistines took him, and put out his eyes, and brought him down to Gaza, and bound him with fetters of brass; and he did grind in the prison house. Howbeit the hair of his head began to grow again after he was shaven.

—Judges 16:18–22

Few people, if any, have lived a life that represented more wasted potential than did Samson. Here was a man who had so much going for him, so much given to him, and yet he squandered it and wasted it. He threw it all away. By the time our text opens, Samson's weakness had caught up with him. His lifestyle had finally cashed the check, and he was brought to the lowest place and point of his life. It is a sad and tragic story. Here he was, the champion of Israel, in a Philistine camp—his eyes gouged out, the laughingstock of the people he was born to destroy. It did not have to end this way for Samson. And Samson's end does not have to be our end, either.

This is a sad story and it would be even sadder were it not for verse 22 in Judges 16, which says, "Howbeit the hair of his head began to grow again."

What a word!

What a statement!

What a promise!

What a God!

In spite of what Samson did to himself, God turned it around and gave him another chance. A lot of us are here today because of the God of second chances. We wouldn't be alive today, we wouldn't be saved today, were God not a God of mercy, a God of grace, and a God of compassion.

The only reason many of us are still here is that God didn't let the enemy triumph over us. What your enemy meant for evil, God made work out for your good. People counted you out; they said it was over and done for—stick a fork in you, you're done. But aren't you glad that God has the last word?

God brought you out in spite of what the devil tried to do to you. God gets the last word. God is still in control. And God deals with us in mercy, grace, and compassion even when we don't deserve it.

All of us have a weakness. You've got a weakness, and I've got a weakness. All of God's children have weaknesses. If it were not for the grace of God, our weakness would become wickedness—but God watches over us.

Samson's life story was one of weakness for women. Every time he saw a woman he wanted her. Every woman he saw he had to have, and these women messed up his life. They turned it upside down. He went from bad to worse, and now in the lap of a woman, he got a haircut that would cost him his life. Samson gave in to Delilah's cunning, Delilah's conniving, Delilah's manipulation. He gave in to it and he fell victim to his weakness.

It's one thing to be weak, but it's something else to be wicked.

God wants to help you while you're weak,
...but he'll judge you when you get wicked.
God will help when you struggle,
...but when you excuse your mess or blame things on others, he will judge you.
God will help you in your weakness,
...but he'll smite you in your wickedness.

Samson had been playing around all day. And now he ended up in the lap of Delilah, getting his hair cut. And then he ended up in a Philistine jail—blind, broken, bruised, battered. But his hair started growing again.

In spite of what you've been through, God is a God of restoration. **Maybe the devil is**

beating you up,
accusing you and attacking you,
telling you that you're not going to make it,
telling you that you're never going to survive,
telling you that you're not going to come out,
telling you that you're never going to get where God is trying to take you.

But the devil is a liar. Philippians 1:6 says that God will complete the good work he has begun in you. If your heart is right and your motives are pure—if you really mean it—then God will restore you.

God restored Samson after his weakness had done him in. But we should not think that restoration is something flippant or casual—"I'm drinking and I'm smoking, and I'm boozing and I'm drugging, but I'm going to get restored." It is foolish to play with God! God will restore you, but don't take him for granted. Don't think you can make God a fool and do what you want to do and then claim restoration.

I believe in a restoring God because I myself am a *recipient* of the restoration of God.

It's a Process

Restoration is a process. Samson's hair didn't grow back overnight. He didn't go to bed a blunder and wake up a wonder. He didn't get a haircut in the wrong barber shop, tell God the next day, "I'm sorry," and then have God give him an instant weave. He didn't lay down that night bald-headed and wake up with seven locks down to his shoulders.

The Bible says there came a point where Samson's hair *began* to grow again. When you and I understand this, it becomes both a source of hope and also a warning: *hope* that restoration can happen but a *warning* not to presume that it will happen overnight. Samson's hair *began* to grow.

Remember, Samson was blind; he couldn't see his hair growing. But his enemies must not have noticed it, either. If they saw it growing real fast, they would have remembered the reason they cut it off in the first place, and they would have given him another haircut. God let it start growing and they didn't even notice. There's some stuff God is doing in your life, but he's doing it so quietly! And he's doing it so slowly that your enemies don't even know it. And by the time they realize it, it's going to be too late.

Restoration is a *process*. You might point out that God forgives us when we confess our sin. Yes, he does. Forgiveness is instantaneous. If you mess up right now and ask God, he'll forgive you right now. But I'm talking about *restoration*. And the problem is, too many of us settle for forgiveness but don't press into restoration.

I don't want God to just forgive me for my mess. I want him to cleanse me. I want him to reposition me so that I can go where he wants me to go in *spite* of my mess. I'm trying to get back. I know I'm forgiven, but

I want my joy back!

I want my anointing back!

I want my power back!

I want my praise back!

I know I'm forgiven. I want *restoration*.

The text tells us that the hair on Samson's head *began* to grow again. Don't rush the process. Some of you are trying too soon, too hard. You want to be right back out in front again. But we can't do that. We love you. God will not be rushed when it comes to your restoration. He will put you on the back burner, put you on hold. He's in no hurry. You might be in a hurry. But God is not in a hurry.

God may have to humble us as a part of our restoration. I don't think God always causes the situation, but I'm convinced that God lets us suffer through some things so he can humble us. Because it's only when we have been humbled that he can really get our attention.

God is in no hurry, and he wants to humble us through the process of restoration. His ultimate goal is to heal us. God lets your hair *begin* to grow. He doesn't do an instant weave. You don't sit in a chair and he weaves it in. No, God "slow-walks" you because he wants to heal you.

Too many folks come back from stuff before they get healed. And because they were never healed, they can't help anyone else. Every time I go and try to help you, something reminds me of what I went through, and since I'm not healed that place is still tender. So while I'm trying to help you, I need help myself because I'm trying to help you from an unhealed place in my own life. But what if I allow God the time he needs to humble me so that he can heal me? Once I get healed then I will be able to help you because I can testify to you that there's life on the other side of your situation.

You may have been through some of the worst imaginable experiences of your life.

This stuff rocked your world,
it buckled your knees,
it made you wonder where in the world you're going
and what's happening.

But you hung on to God, and God healed you over time. And now you can tell somebody else, "I've been there and I've done that. And if you just trust God, he'll bring you through." But you can't say it until you let God do that work in you.

Stop running so fast and getting ahead of God.

Wait until your joy comes back.
Wait until your power comes back.
Wait until your strength comes back.

People won't even know what happened to you, because you let the restoration process play out.

God allowed Samson's hair to grow back slowly and gradually. In fact, we could say that it was *imperceptible*. I love that word. It was unobvious. Samson's hair just started growing again. I want to tell you that even if you can't see it, you are starting to grow again too. Here's how you can tell. You're not crying yourself to sleep every night anymore. Now it's only three nights a week, where it used to be seven. You're not consumed by it anymore. You can go three or four hours and not even think about it. And now when you do think about it, it doesn't sting as bad as it used to.

God is healing you. You're starting to grow again. What you have to do is learn how to shout right where you are, and thank God for the growth that you're having right now. You can't see it, but you're growing.

Every time I used to visit my hometown of New York, I would go to Rockville Cemetery and stop by all the graves: my grandma, my grandpa, my mommy, Mom and Dad Cray, Mom and Pop Kelly. I would go to all the graves and I'd stand there thinking about how much I loved these people, how much I appreciated them, and how much I missed them. Then one time I was in town for a revival, and I asked my friend to take me to the cemetery. He didn't want to go, but I kept insisting, so we finally went. I did my usual thing, visiting all the graves and just standing there. When I was finally ready to leave, the Holy Ghost said to me, "Make this the last time you come here unless they are bringing *you* here."

I said, "What?!"

The Holy Ghost said, "You stop coming here. They are not here. Why do you keep coming here? This is the last time. Go on with your life." And I have not been back to Rockville Cemetery since then.

When I got in the car I told my friend, "Guess what God said? He told me to stop coming to the cemetery."

My friend said, "Praise the Lord!" Because every year he would be my driver to the cemetery.

Perhaps *you* need to make this the last time. You have been living in the graveyard of some bitter disappointments and failures. But God is reviving you and resurrecting you. You were not made to live in the cemetery; you were made to live life. Get out of the cemetery and experience restoration.

It's Painful

Restoration is painful. We often see the finished product, not knowing and never realizing the process that happened behind the scenes and the pain that went with it. Sometimes we don't see true, genuine repentance or restoration in people because we don't let them feel the *pain* of restoration. In Samson's restoration process, they gouged out his eyes. Have you ever been hit in the eye? It is one of the most sensitive parts of your body.

I remember one time I was playing ball and a guy made a throw to me. I went to catch it, but I was blinded by the sun and that baseball hit me right in the eye. I buckled. It hurt. Can you imagine having your eyes gouged out? They gouged out Samson's eyes. And God didn't stop them.

The process of restoration is painful. And we have allowed too many Christians to avoid the pain necessary for restoration. There is a point, and a place, and a period, where you ought to feel bad. When you sin, you ought to feel bad. And it's not others' job to take the pain away. "Baby, don't worry about it. The Lord is good! Baby, don't worry about that. You just confess that and get over it. It's all right!" No, no. There is pain associated with genuine restoration. In fact, you won't be sorry if you don't feel the pain. And you haven't really repented until you have felt godly sorrow.

When I realize that I have failed God, it hurts me. And let me tell you a little secret: I know God doesn't deserve that—not from me. Some people feel that they did God a favor when they got saved. So they can hurt God and it's okay, because after all, they did him a favor. But I know where God brought me from—how unworthy I was, how undeserving I was, how nobody in Far Rockaway expected me to amount to anything. And for God to bring me all the way from that to where I am now, and then for me to think that I have failed him—that breaks my heart! I'm scared of people who can fail God and it does not bother them.

It's painful to realize we have failed God, and it's also painful when we fail others—to know that people believed in you and had faith in you, and you let them down. Sometimes I look at my young grandson and think how much he loves me and looks up to me as his grandpa. And I think, "Lord, help me not to mess up because I don't want him to ever be ashamed that I'm his grandpa." It's a whole other level of responsibility when somebody loves you unconditionally and puts absolute faith in you. You don't want to let that person down. And if you do, it breaks your heart.

There is even pain when you fail yourself. I wasn't there with Samson. I can only imagine what must have gone through his mind during those long hours sitting in that Philistine jail cell. He had days and nights to think about what he had thrown away. He had weeks and months to remember the potential that he had wasted.

How do you live with failing yourself? That's where you might be right now. You have fallen so short of your dreams, of where you said you wanted to be by this season in your life, and you have failed yourself. But that is part of the pain of restoration. In fact, you really can't get restored until you embrace the pain.

It Carries a Price

Restoration is not just a process and it's not just painful, it carries a price.
An old preacher once said that sin will

take you further than you planned to go,

keep you longer than you planned to stay,

and charge you more than you planned to pay.

For Samson, his restoration cost him his life. His hair grew back, but do you know what happened to him in the end? He died with the Philistines. He died with the people he was born to destroy.

Restoration carries a price. Sometimes you are broken inside. You know that you've failed, and your spirit is crushed. You wonder if your heart will ever beat with joy again. Sometimes you are broken physically. You can't just drink liquor and do drugs and have it not take a toll on your body. You can't just give yourself to everybody and your heart not be wounded and scarred. You can't just live capriciously and casually and your spirit not be damaged by it.

Sin always costs you. It will take a toll on you. Samson was lying on a bunk in a Philistine jail because of the sin in his life. But that's not the whole story. While he was lying there, his hair started growing. It never grew back to the full length that it was before. It was never seven locks of black, shiny hair again. It was just a little bit—but it was enough for God to use Samson one more time.

You may have gotten saved when you were 60, and you don't have the strength you did when you were 20 or 30. But that's all right, because the God I serve is able to use you at 60.

He couldn't get you at 20,

and he couldn't get you at 30,

but he'll take you when you come and get some good out of your life.

You may have drunk all your life. Now your liver is shot and your nerves are bad, but the God I serve is still able to take shaking hands and messed-up livers and do something with them. You may have taken drugs all your life and you're all broken and bruised, but the God I serve can take bruised and broken people and make miracles out of them.

You don't need all your hair; you just need a little for God to use.

You don't need all your strength.

You don't need all your power.

You don't need all your ability.

Because little becomes much when you place it in the Master's hands.

You can come to Jesus just as you are, with every failure and every issue. In him you will find a resting place.

He will pick you up.

He will clean you up.

He will turn you around.

He will give you another chance.

Jesus will put

running in your feet,

clapping in your hands,

joy in your soul,

and peace in your mind.

I've been wounded, but my hair is starting to grow again, and I feel my strength coming back. I will bless the Lord at all times. I've been through the storm and I've been through the rain, but I'm still standing by the grace of God.

He will fix it for you,

he will make a way where there is no way,
he will give you another chance,
he will restore.
I fell down,
...but I got back up.
I messed up,
...but God gave me another chance.
I failed,
...but God picked me up, turned me around,
and placed my feet on solid ground.

Samson's hair began to grow again. It never grew all the way, but it grew enough for God's purposes. And whatever time you have left in this life—whatever little bit of strength you have—God can take it and use it and make something powerful.

Let Samson be a reminder to you and to me. God does restore—but not without a process, not without some pain, and not without a price.

CHAPTER 6:

When You Are Used (Leah)

> And Laban said unto Jacob, Because thou art my brother, shouldest thou therefore serve me for nought? tell me, what shall thy wages be? And Laban had two daughters: the name of the elder was Leah, and the name of the younger was Rachel. Leah was tender eyed; but Rachel was beautiful and well favoured. And Jacob loved Rachel; and said, I will serve thee seven years for Rachel.... And Laban said, It is better that I give her to thee, than that I should give her to another man: abide with me. And Jacob served seven years for Rachel.... And Jacob said unto Laban, Give me my wife, for my days are fulfilled, that I may go in unto her. And Laban gathered together all the men of the place, and made a feast. And it came to pass in the evening, that he took Leah his daughter, and brought her to him; and he went in unto her.... And it came to pass, that in the morning, behold, it was Leah: and he said to Laban, What is this thou hast done unto me? did not I serve with thee for Rachel? . . . And Laban said, It must not be so done in our country, to give the younger before the firstborn. Fulfil her week, and we will give thee this also for the service

which thou shalt serve with me yet seven other years. And Jacob did so, and fulfilled her week: and he gave him Rachel his daughter to wife also.... And he went in also unto Rachel, and he loved also Rachel more than Leah, and served with him yet seven other years. —Genesis 29:15–30

What a story! Did you notice what happened to Jacob here? The old switcheroo. Jacob didn't figure out what had happened until he woke up in the morning. But remember, the text says that it was evening—it was dark. There were no electric lights back in those days, just candles. When they blew the candle out, it was pitch black. There weren't any streetlights.

When it was dark, it was dark.

It was as dark as ten thousand midnights in a cypress swamp.

It was dark, all right.

So when Jacob woke up the next morning, he discovered that it was Leah in the bed with him.

Do you realize that Jacob probably did not really say, "What is this thou hast done unto me?" Come on, get real! The Bible cleaned that up. That is not what he said. Jacob was enraged at Laban: "I worked seven years for Rachel! Why would you trick me like this?" But Laban told Jacob that it was not their custom to marry off a younger daughter ahead of the firstborn.

There was enough trickery to go around here. Jacob knew what the custom was. What he was asking his father-in-law, Laban, to do was just ignore what was supposed to be done. He knew. This wasn't some special rule in Laban's family. It was the order of the day. And even though Laban agreed to let Rachel marry Jacob, he never intended to keep that commitment.

When you've got two tricky folks, you've got a mess on your hands:

both of them tricking each other,

both of them lying to each other,

both of them trying to outsmart the other.

Jacob knew when he asked for Rachel that this would be out of order. And Laban knew when he said yes that he wasn't going to follow through. They both knew that they were incorrect.

Jacob said, "I worked seven years to get Rachel! What do you mean by this trickery?"

Laban told him, "That's not the way we do it here. The firstborn gets married first. So wait until Leah's bridal week is over and you can have Rachel too. We'll just throw her in—that is, if you promise to work another seven years for me, wink, wink." Tricky, tricky! So Jacob agreed to work seven more years. He did get Rachel after the first week. He slept with her, too, and he loved her more than Leah.

Wow, both of these women wanted the same man! Two sisters, thrown into a situation not of their own doing. Nowhere before this incident is there any mention of conflict between Rachel and Leah. We're not told that they were having cat fights every night. The Bible tells us that Joseph's brothers hated him from the time he was a kid. It tells us that Jesus' brothers didn't believe in him. We are told in the Bible when there's sibling rivalry and when it starts early. The Bible deals with that. But it never says that Rachel and Leah couldn't get along. They got along just fine until Jacob showed up. These two sisters loved each other. They were happy with each other until Jacob came between them, until they started competing for the affection and the attention of a man.

The Issue of Self-Image

Many women struggle with their own self-image. I can only imagine what it must have been like to be Leah, and to always have yourself described with a "but" connected to your name:

She's nice, but...

She's smart, but...

She's got a nice personality...but her sister, have you seen her sister?

For the sake of self-image, many women will often do things that go against their own self-interest. We see this happen and we just rationalize it. We see them do it and we say, "Aw, that's just the nurturing side, the kind side of a woman. All women are nurturers. That's just the mother instinct." But the stuff some women do is not motherly. Some of their actions, some of their behavior—it's just not nurturing. In fact, it's unhealthy.

Leah and Rachel did stuff against their own self-interest. If you read on in the story, it says that, because Leah was unloved, God let her have children, while Rachel remained barren. And things continued to get worse. Later on they started letting Jacob have children by their maids. All of this over a man! It was bad enough that Leah was just shooting out babies. But then because Rachel couldn't have any, she hooked Jacob up with her maid. Then Leah saw that, so she hooked him up with her own maid. It's all a big mess.

So now Jacob is going between both houses, and the wives are swapping days. He's sleeping with Rachel one day, and then Leah the next. And one day the girls meet in the yard and Leah has some mandrakes from the field and Rachel wants some and so she tells Leah, "I'll let Jacob sleep with you tonight if you give me some mandrakes," and Leah agrees. These girls are having babies; they're letting their husband sleep with other women. And none of that was in their self-interest.

You might be saying, "I would never do anything against my self-interest like Leah and Rachel did, anything that unhealthy!" But you bought that guy a car. You signed for a car for him and then he quit you, and you've still got to pay the note. You signed for it with your silly, needy self. You loaned him money. I don't mean no $20. You loaned him a *lot* of money and then he left you, or he started getting with your girlfriend. Women do things that are not in their own self-interest. And oftentimes men are willing participants in it. We derive some kind of perverted pleasure from it.

The only person happy in this story was the man, Jacob. Rachel wasn't happy; she couldn't have children. Leah wasn't happy; she could have a baby a year but she couldn't get love. And they both must have thought, "It doesn't matter how many times I sleep with Jacob or how many babies I have—he is never going to be mine. I can sleep with him, live with him, and have his babies, but a part of him will always belong to someone else."

The only happy person here was Jacob. He was going from pillar to post. He was like the Holy Ghost, going from heart to heart and breast to breast. But none of the women were really happy. They were doing things that weren't in their own self-interest. Men, think of how many times we've let women do that. We've even encouraged it.

What a Woman Needs

Why would women do things against their own self-interest? Because every woman needs three things. Number one, she needs attention. Why else do you all sit up under those top hair dryers for hours on end? Why else? Because you want somebody to say, "You look nice!" (Ladies, if it will make you feel better, men like to receive attention, as well.)

Women also need affection. But in this story, none of the women really got affection. They had physical contact, but none of them got affection. Affection involves love, and the behavior of the men in their lives certainly didn't communicate love.

Also, every woman needs affirmation. Attention, affection, and affirmation—all three of these things become more important to women as they get older.

One time I was on a plane, and I was listening to this lady talk to another lady. I wasn't eavesdropping; it wasn't like I could slip out or go anywhere. This young lady had gone to the restroom, and she was coming back to her seat. She was very attractive and everybody, including women, was taking notice of her. As she sat down, this lady's seat companion said to her, "I remember when people looked at *me* like that. *Nobody* looks at me like that anymore." If you could have heard the resignation in her voice. It was almost as if she were saying, "I don't turn heads anymore. I don't get attention anymore. And I don't know if I'm still a woman."

Think about the difference between men and women here. As men get older, they are considered distinguished-looking. Women get older and they're just old. For a man: "You're gray and you're so distinguished!" For a woman: "Child, you'd better get you some Clairol!"

Attention.
Affection.
Affirmation.

That's why women sometimes do things against their own self-interest. They are willing to risk hurting themselves if it means the possibility of helping with their self-image.

Self-Identity

Women have to find their own self-identity. And the quest to do this has to be *informed*. This means you have to discover who you really are. Most people—both men and women—never take the time to discover who they really are. Have you ever talked to an older person who is starting to get up there in years and knows that he or she may die soon but is just now starting to find purpose and meaning in life?

You don't know how many times I've had people sit in my office and say, "Pastor, life is something! Just about the time I figure out what it's all about, it's time for me to go." I've had so many people say that to me. "After all this time I finally understand myself, but now I don't have much time left." This is always followed by, "If I knew then what I know now..." You've got to take the time to discover yourself.

Finding your self-identity has to be an *internal* thing—it has to come from within. You are never going to get it from anybody else; you have to get it from yourself. I don't care how many people you're with—how many boyfriends or girlfriends you have—what you're really looking for you're not going to get from anybody else. It must be an inside job.

Finding your self-identity has to be informed, it has to be internal, and it has to be *intentional*. There comes a point where you have to make up your mind and say, "The madness ends today." You've got to look at yourself in the mirror and say, "Today's the last day. This is the last time I'm falling for this trick. **This is the last time I'm going to be**

this needy,

this desperate,

this lonely,

***this* whatever.**

I'm not going there again. Even if I don't ever get married, if I don't never have nobody, I'm going to learn to love myself. I'm going to stop hurting myself to make somebody else happy."

Leah was having all these babies. She became pregnant and had a son, became pregnant again and had a son, became pregnant again and had a son. And then she became pregnant one more time and had a son, and she named him Judah, saying, "Now will I praise the LORD" (Genesis 29:35). And then she stopped having children.

Leah had been having all these babies and naming them according to the self-identity she sought from Jacob: "Now my husband will love me! This time he'll want me!" And she finally said, "This is the last time. I'm not naming this baby anything about Jacob. I'm naming him Judah, which means, 'Now I will praise the Lord.' If Jacob can't love me this way then he doesn't have to. I'm going to stop having children to try to get him to love me. I'm having me a Judah, and I'm going to praise God for who I am. And I'm going to love God for who I am."

Leah was all out of shape by now. She had messed her body up pushing out babies, thinking that it would make Jacob love her, that he would want her, that he would be happy. She kept naming them based on *him*. If everything you do is tied to somebody else, you're never going to find your place in God. You've got to have one last baby and name him Judah:

"This is* my *praise.
This isn't about you.
This has nothing to do with you.
This is between me and God."

You have to find that place where it's just you and God—not you and anybody else.

Leah and Rachel were two sisters divided over a man, and their daddy did it to them. Laban knew what he was doing. His language indicates that it was all a business transaction to him. "Let me tell you what you can do. Work for me seven more years, and I'll throw Rachel in. Go ahead and take her, but work for me." It was all economics.

Here were two women, their daddy, and their husband. The two men in Leah and Rachel's lives who should have protected them—the two men in their lives who should have been looking out for them—were the two men who were causing all the conflict between them. We are never told that they didn't get along prior to Jacob showing up. When he came on the scene, they became sibling rivals. **And for the rest of their lives, they were competing against one another and hurting themselves:**

struggling with self-image,

going against their own self-interest,

and trying desperately to find their self-identity.

Someone you care about may have used you for selfish reasons, but it's time for you to stop hurting yourself. It's time for you to stop going through all of this labor pain, going through all of this trial and struggle. It's not going to make that person love you. It's not going to change anything. You've got to praise God for yourself. You do not have to hurt yourself to try to make someone else happy.

CHAPTER 7:

When You Are Ridiculed (Jesus)

> Now the Jew's feast of tabernacles was at hand. [Jesus'] brethren therefore said unto him, Depart hence, and go into Judaea, that thy disciples also may see the works that thou doest. For there is no man that doeth any thing in secret, and he himself seeketh to be known openly. If thou do these things, shew thyself to the world. For neither did his brethren believe in him. —John 7:2–5

Familiarity breeds contempt. Other people can be with you so often and at such a familiar level that they lose all objective perspective on you. When John 7 says that Jesus' own brothers didn't *believe* in him, it uses the Greek word *pisteuó*, which literally means "to have faith" in someone. Not only were they skeptical about the miracles that everyone saw him doing, but they did not believe he was who he claimed to be—the Anointed One of God. **How could they live with Jesus every day,**

taking shelter under the same roof,

eating at the same table,

sleeping in the same room,

and not believe that he was the Son of God? It seems incredible to us, but Jesus' brothers had known him since they were children, and they scoffed at the idea that he was the Savior of the world. They held him in contempt. They ridiculed him.

Your family may do the same when you commit your life to Jesus. The people you love the most—those you want to bring to Christ so they can know the same abundant life that he has given you—may be the most skeptical because they have known you for so long. It will break your heart if they hold you at arm's length and laugh at what you tell them about the Kingdom. They may be the least inclined to believe what you tell them, so you have to be patient and let your life tell the story. That's not easy.

It's painful when Jesus Christ changes your life and your own family doesn't believe it. They look at you sideways because they believe you're the same person you were twenty years ago, ten years ago, or just last month. They say, "Come on, who are you kidding?

We partied together!

We hung out together!

In fact, you were wilder than me!

Now all of a sudden, you tell me that you're 'born again.' Please! I know you better than that. What are you trying to play me for?"

They nudge each other and wink.

They take bets on how long you're going to maintain this "born again" story.

They tell each other, "This won't last long. We know him too well. After all, we grew up together."

When your own brothers and sisters ridicule your faith, you're in good company, because not even Jesus' brothers believed in him. They said, "Why don't you take this on the road, big brother? See if you convince anyone in Jerusalem, because you certainly don't convince us!" What can you do when your own family makes fun of you like that?

Don't Be Discouraged

Notice what Jesus did. First, he did not allow his brothers' ridicule to discourage him. You need to do the same. If you are a person of genuine faith, you cannot allow other people—no matter how close they are—to deter you from what God has called you to do. **Even if your fiercest critics are**

your siblings,

your parents,

or your best friends,

when you know that God has changed your life, you won't let their ridicule crush your spirit. How?

You won't take it personally. When Israel asked for a king, the prophet Samuel moaned to God because they did not trust his leadership anymore. But God said, "Don't worry about it, Samuel. They don't doubt you; they doubt me. They don't disparage you; they disparage me. That's why they want a king." When your family and friends make jokes about your new life in Christ, it's not because they doubt your ability; it's because they doubt *God's* ability. They know what you have done in the past. In their opinion, God cannot possibly forgive and cleanse you of all that. So don't take their ridicule personally. They are not mocking you; they are mocking God.

You won't let their attitude determine yours. You cannot allow what other people say or do determine whether you have joy. If you let them control your joy, you give them more power than they deserve. **You can say,**

"I want you to be happy for me.

I want you to celebrate what God has done for me.

I want you to believe the transformation at work in me.

But if you don't, I am going to praise God anyway. The joy of the Lord is still my strength, and I will bless the Lord at all times because he has redeemed me from the ruined life I had before."

You won't make your pain permanent. The derisive comments of your family and friends may take you by surprise, and they actually "rain on your parade" at first. But that doesn't have to be your permanent frame of mind.

Don't Be Distracted

Notice how Jesus responded when his brothers taunted him to put on a show of miracles in Jerusalem: "Go ye up unto this feast: I go not up yet unto this feast: for my time is not yet full come" (John 7:8). He did not let their ridicule distract him. He knew what God expected him to do, and he would not let anything deter him—not even the desire to set his kid brothers straight!

Jesus did not let ridicule distract him from his *path*. God gives every one of us a life path that will develop our spiritual gifts to the maximum extent and enable us to bring the most glory to him. A lot of us would be much further along that path if we had not turned aside to prove ourselves to skeptical family and friends.

Jesus did not allow ridicule to distract him from his *purpose*. "My time is not yet full come," he said. He knew the assignment his heavenly Father had given him, and he would not be dissuaded by criticism from his earthly family. When you know why God has created you, when you are certain of what God wants you to do, you won't allow anyone to pull you aside—not even your parents or siblings.

Ridicule did not distract Jesus from his *project*. He was as task-oriented as Nehemiah when he rebuilt the wall of Jerusalem. Nehemiah's enemies sent messengers to him four times, demanding that he meet them on the field of battle, but he said, "I am doing a great work, so that I cannot come down: why should the work cease, whilst I leave it, and come down to you?" (Nehemiah 6:3). Too often, when God gives us a project, we let ourselves be distracted by what other people are saying about our project.

What you are doing for God is more important than anything you might do for someone else. **Do not allow**

criticism,

complaints,

or catcalls from others

to distract you from God's commission.

Don't Be Dissuaded

Jesus would not yield to his brothers' argument. "My time is not yet come: but your time is always ready. The world cannot hate you; but me it hateth, because I testify of it, that the works thereof are evil" (John 7:6–7). In other words, he said, "Do what you want while I do what I must."

I believe this is an important key to serving God: *We don't do what we want; we do what we must.* If we do what we must, God may someday allow us to do what we want; but if we do only what we want, we will never find time to do what we must. Real joy comes from doing what we must do for God, not from doing what we want to do for our own gratification.

Jesus would not be rushed. His brothers said that if he was really the Messiah, he may as well go to the religious center of Israel and begin doing great things. They sounded like well-meaning family members who tell a new Christian, "You look like a preacher. Why don't you start preaching?" But wise servants of God won't be rushed into ministry before they are ready.

Jesus would not risk displeasing God. He would rather please God and displease his brothers any day of the week. Moreover, Jesus would not ruin God's plan for his life. He knew that Calvary was ahead of him. He knew that his Father sent him to redeem the world—including his brothers. He would not spoil that plan by following his brothers' "Plan B."

This is not the only time Jesus' brothers are mentioned in the New Testament. Matthew 12 says that they showed up one day and asked Jesus to curtail a sermon for a little family conference. Someone said, "Behold, thy mother and thy brethren stand without, desiring to speak with thee" (v 47). But Jesus gestured to the listening crowd and responded, "Behold my mother and my brethren!" (v 49). Again, he would not abandon his mission for anyone.

Acts 1 lists several of Jesus' followers who had gathered in an upper room of Jerusalem after his ascension, and concludes, "These all continued with one accord in prayer and supplication, with the women, and Mary the mother of Jesus, and with his brethren" (v 14). Notice the contrast:

John 7 says his brothers didn't believe him,
...but Acts 1 says they were among his disciples in the upper room.
John 7 says they ridiculed his ministry,
...but Acts 1 says they prayed for his ministry to continue.
John 7 says they thought he was deluded,
...but Acts 1 says they thought he was divine.

What happened to Jesus' brothers between John 7 and Acts 1? The same kind of thing that may have to happen to you. For Jesus and his family, the turning point was a place called Calvary on a Good Friday. He had to die on a cross, be buried in a tomb, and be raised from the dead before his family believed he was the Son of God.

You may have to go through the fire before your friends and family believe your faith is real. Something traumatic may happen to you before your disbelieving family changes their minds.

You may have to lose your job and keep your joy
for them to believe in you.
You may have to go through hardship with a "hallelujah"
for them to believe in you.
You may have to die and still dance
for them to believe in you.

Nothing will silence a family's ridicule quite like the testing of your testimony.

When you come through times of trouble with God's praise on your lips, those who wink and snicker at your faith may become believers themselves. You don't want to miss that!

DISCUSSION QUESTIONS

CHAPTER 1: When You Are Rejected (Joseph)

1. Why does rejection cause us so much pain? Why do some people seem to move beyond it rather quickly while others slip into obsession or depression?
2. What are some keys to turning our thoughts so they are not focused on the people who have hurt us?
3. What resources has God placed in your life to help you handle hardship?
4. How have you seen the pain of rejection give birth to a passionate resolve to overcome—either in your own life or in the life of someone else?
5. In the long term, the betrayal of Joseph by his brothers led to great things in Joseph's life. He received blessings and benefits that he never would have known otherwise. How do we see the hand of God at work and maintain our faith when things do not turn out as positively for us as they did for Joseph?

CHAPTER 2: When You Are Broken (Woman with an Issue of Blood)

1. Why do finances seem to be an area where many people—even Christians—struggle and where the Enemy gains a foothold to cause division and discouragement?
2. How are you at managing your money? What resources are available to educate and assist people in this area?
3. Regardless of how much money you have, in what other areas are you "rich"?
4. How committed was the woman in this story to making a connection with Jesus? How committed are you personally to making such a connection? What, if anything, needs to change about that?
5. In reflecting on his childhood and some family struggles from that time, Bishop Clarke identified how God was at work. How has faith been an anchor for you in times and places of brokenness and struggle?

CHAPTER 3: When You Are Shamed (David's Men)

1. David's men were shamed by having half of their beards shaved and having their garments cut off to expose their private parts. In our society, what tends to be viewed as shameful?
2. Sometimes shame is brought on us by others, and sometimes we bring it on ourselves. How is it even possible to have a "false" sense of shame?
3. What has been a place of "retreat" in your life—someplace you could go to catch your breath, regroup, and find the power to return?

4. How do we determine the timeframe for our recovery from shame? How can rushing the process be a bad thing? How can taking too long be a bad thing?
5. Think of a time when you were shamed or hurt. What were the signs that God was healing you and preparing you to make a comeback?

CHAPTER 4: When It's Hard to Let Go (Prodigal Family)

1. What in your life has proven the hardest for you to let go? Why?
2. When has a parent, a boss, or someone else held something back for you that proved to be a great blessing when you finally received it?
3. We often experience brokenness as a consequence of our own poor choices. How is the healing and restoration God offers us in these situations evidence of the love and grace of God?
4. Why does bitterness sometimes seem to take root even in the lives of Christians? How should we respond to fellow believers who are constantly bitter?
5. Even in the areas of your life you would consider to be good right now, how might God have something better in mind for you?

CHAPTER 5: When You Need Restoration (Samson)

1. How do we discern when we might have crossed the line from weakness to wickedness?

2. In what specific areas have you been healed, enabling you to bring help and hope to others who are now struggling with those same things?
3. In what ways do you tend to live in the graveyard of past disappointments and failures, when God is prompting you to move on and experience restoration?
4. When have you failed God, others, or yourself and felt great pain because of it? How can God use the pain of such an experience to move you to repentance and restoration?
5. Regardless of your age and regardless of your past mistakes, what would you like to see God do in and through your life in the years you have left?

CHAPTER 6: When You Are Used (Leah)

1. Even in our own day, why do babies or children sometimes end up being thought of as a "tool" to bring happiness or win affection?
2. Why is there such a double standard between women and men with respect to age and looks?
3. So you don't have to say "If I knew then what I know now..." someday, how can you be more intentional now about finding purpose and meaning in life?
4. What might be helpful in finding that place where it's just you and God—in other words, in praising and loving God for who he has created you to be?
5. In spite of Jacob's behavior with Leah and Rachel, God worked through their children to establish the twelve tribes of Israel. What hope does this give us for the work God might do in our own lives?

CHAPTER 7: When You Are Ridiculed (Jesus)

1. After his boyhood trip to the Temple with his parents (Luke 2:41–52), the Bible gives no other details of Jesus' life until he was about 30. What do you think it was like growing up in the same household as Jesus?
2. How could someone live with Jesus in the flesh and not believe he was the Son of God? How can people today deny the existence of God or the power of the Holy Spirit despite evidence to the contrary?
3. How have nonbelievers in your life responded to your faith in Jesus and your efforts to live as a disciple of Christ?
4. Jesus did not let anything distract him from the work God had for him. What in your life tends to pull you away from the plan and purpose God has for you?
5. Whether a testimony is dramatic or depicts a less drama-filled path to faith, what is it that makes any sort of testimony about coming to faith in Christ powerful?

Bishop Timothy J. Clarke

was called to the ministry in 1974 and first served in his hometown as Associate Minister at First Church of God, Far Rockaway, New York. He began his first pastorate in November of 1977 at the York Avenue Church of God in Warren, Ohio, where he served the congregation for four years. In February of 1982, he was called to be the Senior Pastor of First Church of God in Columbus, Ohio, where he still serves. In 2001, the Lord led Bishop Clarke to create the Berean Fellowship of Churches, which at the present time includes more than 50 congregations of various denominations. He also serves the church-at-large as an evangelist and teacher.

Bishop Clarke received a Master of Ministry degree from the Southern California School of Ministry in Los Angeles, California, and was consecrated to the office of Bishop in 2001. He has been awarded honorary doctorates from Mid-America Christian University, the Southern California School of Ministry, and Wilberforce University, and has been inducted to the Morehouse College Board of Preachers.

After his ordination by the Church of God, Anderson, Indiana, in 1977, Bishop Clarke began a long career of association with the National Association of the Church of God, West Middlesex, Pennsylvania. His service has included President of the National Inspirational Youth Convention; Chairman and Vice-Chairman of the General Assembly; and President, Vice-President, and Presiding Elder of the National Association of the Church of God.

Bishop Clarke is the author of nine previous books: *Signs of His Coming* (1998), *Help for Those Who Hurt* (2001), *Bring Back the Glory* (2001), *Daughter, Don't Miss Your Season* (2002), *Living in the Blessed Place* (2003), *Making the Most of Your Time* (2004), *Celebrating the Family* (2005), *Reclaiming Your Spiritual Health* (2006), and *Paying the Price to Win: Putting Your Faith into Action* (2008).

Timothy Clarke and his wife, the former Clytemnestra Lawson of Teaneck, New Jersey, are the parents of two adult children, Dionesha (Ocie) Clarke-Logan and Joscelyn Renee Clarke, and the proud grandparents of Ryan Joseph Clarke and London Yvonne Logan.

CPSIA information can be obtained
at www.ICGtesting.com
Printed in the USA
FFOW01n1618231016
28711FF

9 781593 178796